ANGER is OKAY
VIOLENCE is NOT

by
Julie K. Federico

Anger is Okay Violence is NOT

Cover and interior design by Elizabeth M. Hawkins
Illustrations by Glori Alexander

Printed in the United States of America

ISBN: 978-1-64516-993-2

Juvenile Nonfiction / Social Issues / Physical & Emotional Abuse

DEDICATION

This book is dedicated to Cathy Bearce—the assistant manager at the TD Ritter Center—and the preschool teachers at the Community Renewal Team Headstart in Hartford, Connecticut, for without your encouragement, this book would not exist.

ACKNOWLEDGEMENT

I would like to acknowledge all of the parents raising children in homes where domestic violence is present. My heart goes out to you. Please get to higher ground. Seek safety for yourself and your children.There is no greater gift you can give them.

"The LORD is close to the brokenhearted; he rescues those whose spirits are crushed."

Psalm 34:18 (NLT)

iNTRODUCTiON

More than five million children witness an act of domestic violence every year.

This is an important book because there's a lack of age-appropriate classroom material that enables children to feel safe enough to talk about hard topics, such as domestic violence. Books like this enable children to look at a scary topic in a safe environment, and give a name to the behaviors and feelings that they are experiencing.

Cathy Bearce
Assistant Unit Manager
Early Care and Education Program
Community Renewal Team
Hartford, Connecticut

Note to Readers

Anger is OKAY Violence is NOT is a book with dual purposes. It is one of the most important books on the market for children living with domestic violence. The second less threatening purpose is to help toddlers manage their anger and temper tantrums. If you are buying this book because you have young children throwing fits daily, hourly consider yourself very fortunate. These problems will self correct much more quickly than the issue of domestic violence. When children gain command of the language and learn a few words this decreases tantrums. I remember when my older daughter learned the two words, "Need help." This helped cut her tantrums in half because it altered me that she needed help with something. I came over and helped her with whatever was giving her problems instead of her screaming at the top of her lungs and throwing whatever it was across the room. With my second child I tried to guide her when she was having a tantrum. If we were checking out from the grocery or at a doctor's appt. I would say, "Don't melt now!" Inferring that if you can give me just five minutes to get out of here wherever here was you can safely melt down later. At first my daughter had no idea what I was talking about. Shortly thereafter as I would plead, "Don't melt now!" she would sometimes fall to the ground in exhaustion and yell; "I am melting now!" Other times she would lift her arms up to be held and my closeness to her helped us buy the precious five minutes we needed to leave and melt down in privacy.

This book also teaches replacement behaviors. Like kicking a bad smoking habit if an adult says to a child, "Cut it out! Stop!" without offering a replacement behavior the parent's demands will go usually unnoticed by the child. If you say to your toddler, "No, you can not throw the ball at your 2 week old brother but you can go outside and throw the ball up against the wall or play catch with me." This will go further with redirecting them. If you tell someone not to smoke without offering a replacement behavior there is little chance for success. Replacement behaviors are non-violent, safe, and appropriate activities for your child. When they get older and you have used this language with them you can tell them. "That won't work, you need to find a replacement behavior." Over time children will have a list of behaviors they can pull from at a moment's notice. Toddlers need skills to deal with anger and language to help them express what they are feeling when the tantrum strikes. This book will help with that. It is best not to read the book mid or post tantrum but on a calm morning when everyone is well rested.

Tantrums do end and this book will help them end sooner, then you will be greeted with yet another parenting challenge after you master tantrums. Ah, the road to adulthood is never smooth.

If you are buying this book because you and your children are living with domestic violence I am very sorry. No one deserves to go through the horrors of domestic violence except a perpetrator of domestic violence so they can see what it is like to be on the receiving end of violence. Please seek support from trained professionals. I would be very careful which family and friends you self disclose to because some people can do more harm than good to you after you share your story. You are intuitive and will know who is a safe person and who is not. The fact that you are holding this book is a celebration! It is a celebration because you are looking for resources and trying the best way you know how to send your children a lifeline. Be proud of yourself for this, your children will benefit from this more that you will ever know. All school personnel are mandatory reporters that is why I choose the fish in the story to resemble a teacher. Although when confronting domestic violence reporting is not your largest issue. Reporting takes approximately one hour of your time or less. The issue is: Do you want live with more abuse in the years to come or do you want to leave and rebuild your life? Neither are easy. But if you stay long term the damage that will be done to you and your children will be irreparable. If you are one of the fortunate victims of domestic violence who has physical evidence left on their body after a domestic violence episode you will fare better in court if this evidence is documented with a police report. If you are the less fortunate as I was and there are no marks or physical evidence your road will more challenging if you are going through the court system. The good news is that you can leave your abuser and never file a court document about the abuse unless you choose to. I say these things with a great deal of compassion and understanding. I was in a marriage where domestic violence was present for almost 9 years. For the last 11 years I have been dealing with domestic violence in a non-direct way as my abuser has used the court system to carry out his continued abuse. I share this information so that you know it can be done, it is possible to leave an abuser and rebuild.

Children are so delicate they encounter abuse on a completely different level that adults do. Their DNA are easily imprinted. If you have boys and they are witnessing domestic violence you are grooming them to become abusers when they reach adulthood. If you have daughters you are teaching them daily that abuse is okay and that you sanction it. I know you do not agree with the abuse however your actions of staying in an abusive relationship sanction it even if your words would declare otherwise. No dialogue has to be spoken about either of these things. Children learn from their environment even when parents do not use any words or language. It is strange and very scary. The best thing for your children is for them to grow up in a violence free house. If you can not call and report the abuse have your children tell someone anyone at school that they are being harmed. Leaving domestic violence is not easy; staying is even harder and more damaging for children. I think each year you live in a home where domestic violence is not present you add two years onto your life. Thank you for finding my book and reading my message. God's speed, please get to higher ground. Lastly, you are not alone according to the Childhood Domestic Violence Association, 5 million children a year in the United States witness acts of domestic violence." http://cdv.org/2014/02/10-startling-domestic-violence-statistics-for-children/

I have not sold 5 million books yet so I know more people need to hear this message. After you are done with the book will you donate it to a school, daycare, library, church or share it with a friend? This will keep the information moving around in a positive way. Thank you.

Julie Federico
June 2017

Everyone gets angry. Even fish get angry.

It is okay to be angry

as long as you are not hurting anyone.

Is it okay to push someone when you are angry?

Is it okay to throw something when you are angry?

Is it okay to bite someone when you are angry?

If someone in your family is angry and hurting others, is it the fault of the younger fish?

NO!

What if the younger fish left seaweed snacks in the back of the boat?
Is it okay for the adult fish to hurt them?

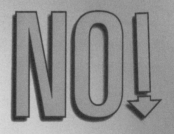

NO!

Is it okay to paint a picture when you are angry?

YES!

Is it okay to play soccer when you are angry?

YES!↓

Is it okay to cry when you are angry?

YES!⬇

YES!↓

It is okay to be angry
as long as you are not hurting anyone.

YES!↓

If someone in your family is getting angry
and hurting others, it is okay to tell your
teacher or another trusted adult.

Everyone gets angry, and this is okay. But it is not okay to get angry and hurt people.

If someone you know is hurting others when they are angry, tell a trusted adult.

Anger should not hurt others.

This subject is so important and often gets overlooked in the planning of lesson plans. According to the Childhood Domestic Violence Association, over 5 million children a year in the United States witness acts of domestic violence. http://cdv.org/2014/02/10- startling-domestic-violence-statistics-for-children/

These children litter your classrooms and chiefly remain silent to the violence they witnessed. I am trying to change this one book at a time. Children deserve to grow up in a violence free home.

Objective:
Students will increase their awareness around anger and anger issues. Students will learn what to do if someone in their family has explosive anger. Students will learn replacement skills instead of outward anger.

Read *Anger is OKAY Violence is NOT* to students.

Have students give some feedback. What was your favorite part of the book? What is one question that you have for the author?

Everyone gets angry right? Right!

Give an example of the last time you got angry or have students share an example. What happened when you got angry what did you do?

Talk about replacement behaviors. Replacement behaviors are things students can do besides rage. For example drawing, painting, writing poetry, crying, talking to a friend. Ask students for their favorite replacement behavior activity. Possibly share yours.

In the story where the father fish got furious when the kids spilt snacks in the back of his boat. Ask the students if they think this behavior is okay? Ask students if they ever see this type of behavior from adults their own family.

If student's self-disclose that violent anger is happening to them talk with them privately at another time possible with the school counselor or social worker present.

Recap that anger is okay, everyone gets angry, but anger should not hurt others. Read the book more than once. It takes more than one lesson for these ideas to set in with students.

If you don't know who to get help from, you can call **National Domestic Violence Hotline** for free at 1-800-799-SAFE (7233) or TTY 1-800-787-3224. https://www.thehotline.org/

domesticshelters.org
www.domesticshelters.org
Theresa's Fund/DomesticShelters.org
PO Box 32695
Phoeniz, AZ 85064

National Coalition Against Domestic Violence
One Broadway Suite B210
Denver, CO 80203
(303) 839-1852
http://www.ncadv.org/

CPSIA information can be obtained
at www.ICGtesting.com
Printed in the USA
LVHW010855121120
671500LV00005B/158

9 781645 169932